Aim to be a midfield star? Then listen up!

You need to boss the ball.

Keep it under control.

Check out these cool skills.

You need to learn to pass well. A quick pass can be a winning pass.

The pass can be short …

or long …

or you can chip it.

The match can be won in midfield.

So keep sharp,
sure and bright!

You will need to learn to control the ball ...

with your feet ...

or with your thigh.

Or you can control it with your chest.

But whatever you do, just keep the ball ...

and pass it straight. Just relax
and you will do well.

Midfield stars are real winners.

Are you?